First Peoples

Later Contact

Pearson Australia
(a division of Pearson Australia Group Pty Ltd)
707 Collins Street, Melbourne, Victoria 3008
PO Box 23360, Melbourne, Victoria 8012
www.pearson.com.au

First published 2012 by Pearson Australia
2015 2014 2013
10 9 8 7 6 5 4 3

Author: Liz Flaherty
Consultant: Lyn Beasley
Commissioning Editor: Sabine Bolick
Project Editor: Rachel Davis
Editor: Beth Zeme
Designers: Anne Donald and Jennifer Johnston
Copyright & Pictures Editor: Katy Murenu
Cover Designer: Glen McClay
Printed in Australia by the SOS Print + Media Group

National Library of Australia Cataloguing-in-Publication entry
Author: Flaherty, Liz, 1963-
Title: Later contact / Liz Flaherty.
ISBN: 978 1 4425 5990 5 (pbk.)
Series: First peoples.
Notes: Includes index.
Target Audience: For primary school age.
Subjects: Aboriginal Australians – Australia – History – Juvenile literature.
Torres Strait Islanders – Australia – History – Juvenile literature.
Europeans – Australia – History – Juvenile literature.
Immigrants – Australia – History – Juvenile literature.
Australia – Ethnic relations – History – Juvenile literature.

Dewey Number: 305.89915

Pearson Australia Group Pty Ltd ABN 40 004 245 943

Acknowledgements
We would like to thank the following for permission to reproduce copyright material. The following abbreviations are used in this list: t = top, b = bottom, l = left, r = right, c = centre.

AAP: William West, p. 19t. AIATSIS: © Aboriginal Studies Press, AIATSIS. No reproduction allowed without permission, p. 7t. Astro Photography: Roger Groom, p. 23b. Battye Library, State Library of Western Australia: Courtesy of Royal Western Australian Historical Society, p. 19b. Carroll and Richardson Flagworld: Carroll and Richardson Flagworld Pty Ltd – Worldwide licence to exclusively print the Aboriginal flag © Harold Thomas, pp. 21t, 29cl. Commonwealth of Australia: Apology speech text, p. 19. Corbis Australia: Cannon Collection, p. 13. Fairfax: Jim McEwen, pp. 17, 29t; Jason South, p. 23t. Frank Allen: Painting reproduced with permission from Frank Allen: www.frankallen.com.au, p. 28. Getty Images: Mark Dadswell, p. 27; Hulton Archive, p. 15b; Penny Tweedie, p. 5; Simon Wilkinson, p. 7b. Love, Lawry: p. 8. Mitchell Library, State Library of New South Wales: ML27, p. 9. National Library of Australia: nla.pic-an23378504, p. 11. Newspix: Sean Davey, p. 16. Pearson Australia: Alice McBroom, p. 25. Shutterstock: Del Monaco, p. 24; FlashStudio, p. 29b; Robyn Mackenzie, p. 15t. Torres Strait Island Regional Council (TSIRC): With permission from Torres Strait Island Regional Council (TSIRC) and Mr Bernard Namok, pp. 21b, 29cr.

Every effort has been made to trace and acknowledge copyright. However, if any infringement has occurred, the publishers tender their apologies and invite the copyright holders to contact them.

Some of the images used in *First Peoples: Later Contact* might have associations with deceased Indigenous Australians. Please be aware that these images might cause sadness or distress in Aboriginal or Torres Strait Islander communities.

Contents

Words that are printed in bold are explained in the Glossary on page 30.

Introduction

This series of books is about the first peoples who lived in Australia. It explores their arrival, their culture and lifestyles and their contact with Europeans.

First Peoples

Australia is an **ancient continent**. It has been inhabited continuously for many thousands of years. Aboriginal and Torres Strait Islander peoples lived in Australia long before the arrival of Europeans.

Aboriginal peoples live across the whole continent of Australia. Traditionally, Torres Strait Islander peoples lived on the islands in the Torres Strait, which is between the Cape York Peninsula on mainland Australia and New Guinea.

Aboriginal and Torres Strait Islander peoples are not one group of people. There are many different groups or nations. Each group has its own culture, customs and language. It has been estimated that over 250 different languages were spoken by Aboriginal groups across Australia before European arrival.

About this Book

This book explores what happened to Aboriginal and Torres Strait Islander peoples after the arrival of the First Fleet in 1788.

Life for Australia's Indigenous peoples changed forever when Europeans arrived to occupy Australia. Relations between European settlers and Indigenous peoples were strained from the outset, but worsened over the 19th and 20th centuries.

However, the situation has improved in the 21st century. Australia is learning to embrace its Indigenous peoples and respect their traditions and culture. Unfortunately, problems continue with the health, **life expectancy**, education and welfare of Indigenous peoples compared to other Australians.

Culture and traditions are still important to Aboriginal and Torres Strait Islander peoples today.

European Arrival

Before the First Fleet arrived in 1788, it is estimated that between 500 000 and 1 million Aboriginal and Torres Strait Islander peoples lived in Australia. They respected the land, plants and animals that provided them with food, clothing and shelter.

The 19th Century

Within a few years of European arrival, Aboriginal peoples, particularly in New South Wales, were forced from their own lands and were treated with disrespect, fear and often hatred. By the start of the 19th century, just 12 years after contact with the new arrivals, the Aboriginal population was **decimated**. Many people died from diseases that they had never been exposed to before, and a large number of people were killed by European settlers.

The landscape also changed greatly. Large areas of land were cleared and animals that were once **abundant** became scarce. Europeans also introduced plants and animals that were not native to Australia. Some of the plants, such as blackberries, and animals, such as rabbits, cats and foxes, have caused terrible damage.

Alfred Canning

Some Aboriginal people living in the Great Sandy Desert in Western Australia only met Europeans in 1906, when Alfred Canning began searching there for a stock route and sources of water. This route became known as the Canning Stock Route. Canning has been very much criticised for his treatment of Aboriginal people.

Languages

Of the estimated 250 different Aboriginal and Torres Strait Islander languages spoken in 1788, many have now disappeared. While approximately 145 languages are spoken today, only about 18 languages are still spoken fluently and taught to children.

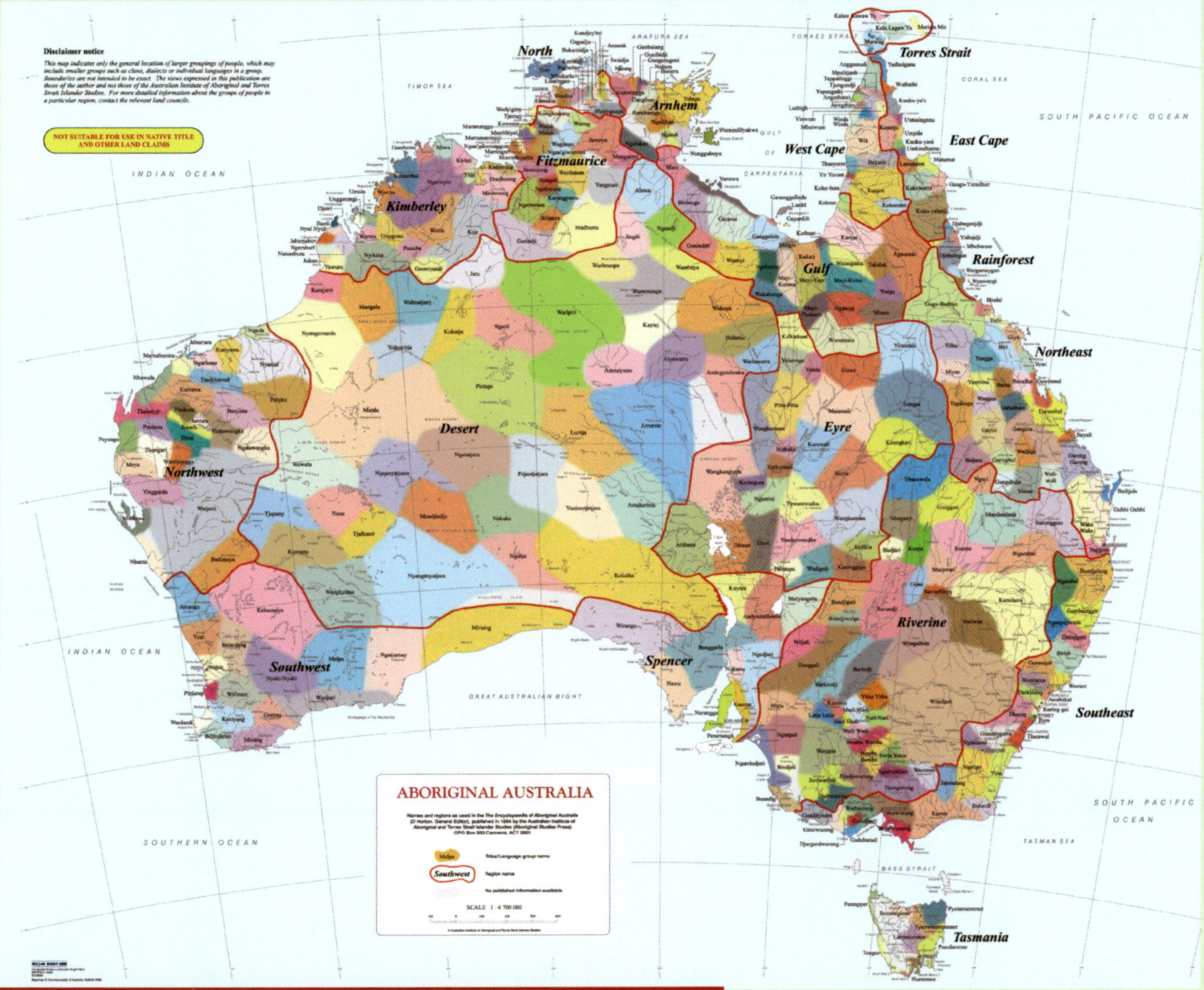

This map shows the Aboriginal and Torres Strait Islander nation groups, or language groups.

Great Sandy Desert, Western Australia

Tasmania

Some of the harshest mistreatment of Aboriginal people occurred when Europeans spread to Tasmania. Only 30 years after the arrival of Europeans, the Tasmanian Aboriginal population was almost wiped out through disease and **massacres**.

Martial Law

Before European contact, between 5000 and 10 000 Aboriginal people lived in Tasmania. In 1828, only an estimated few hundred remained. Still, the government declared Martial Law against the remaining Aboriginal people, meaning the settlers could shoot them on sight.

In 1830, a five-pound **bounty** was put on Aboriginal adults brought in to the government alive and a two-pound bounty on Aboriginal children. Aboriginal people were **outlawed** in their own Country because European people wanted their land.

The Black Line

The **campaign** to get rid of the Tasmanian Aboriginal peoples from 1803 to 1832 was called the Black War.

In 1830, the government called upon every European person in Tasmania to form a line across the country. The aim was to catch and kill the remaining Aboriginal people during a three-week period.

This became known as the Black Line. Only one man and boy were captured. However, the line did force people out of their homelands.

This painting by Lawry Love called "Colonisation" shows some of the harsh ways Aboriginal peoples were treated.

The Bruny Island mission was led by George Robinson.

Mission

A **mission** was set up to house Tasmania's Aboriginal people on Bruny Island, off the Tasmanian coast. Here, the Aboriginal people were banned from speaking their own languages and practising ceremonies that were very important to them. They were taught Christianity rather than their own spiritual beliefs.

Truganini

Truganini was born on Bruny Island in 1812. By the time she was 17, her mother, uncle and the man she was to marry had been murdered, and her sister had been kidnapped by seal hunters.

Spokesperson

Truganini tried to help her people by being a **spokesperson** for them. The **mission** on Bruny Island was to shut down because of the number of deaths from European diseases, against which the Aboriginal people had no resistance. Truganini negotiated with George Robinson to get the best outcome for her people.

Three hundred Aboriginal people moved to a new mission on Flinders Island, where the government promised they would be safe and that they would be allowed to return to their homeland later.

Back to the Mainland

There were many deaths from European diseases at the Flinders Island mission as well.

In 1847, the government moved the last 47 people left in the mission back to the Tasmanian mainland. However, the Aboriginal people were forced to live in a deserted convict station. They were not allowed to return to their homelands as the government had promised.

After a short time, only three people remained alive. Truganini was the last person from the mission to die in 1876.

Tasmania Today

Fortunately, some Aboriginal people escaped the missions and lived in small communities both on the mainland and on other islands in Bass Strait. Their **ancestors** today are very proud of their Tasmanian Aboriginal **heritage**.

In 1904, Truganini's body was put on display in the Tasmanian Museum and samples of her hair and skin were sent to Britain. It was only in 1976 that her body was finally returned to her people. Her hair and skin were returned from Britain in 2002.

Coranderrk

In Victoria, the Aboriginal population before 1835 was estimated to be 11 500 people. By 1857, there were less than 2000 Aboriginal people. When European people took over the land of Aboriginal people for their farms and towns, there was nowhere for them to go.

Coranderrk

Simon Wonga of the Wurundjri **clan reclaimed** a portion of land near Healesville in Victoria. In 1863, Wonga and his cousin, William Barak, led 40 people back to their Country and formed a settlement called Coranderrk. With the help of their friend Pastor John Green, they **petitioned** the government for ownership of this land.

Even though they had less than one per cent of their original land, the station was very successful for many years, producing wheat, hops and craft items for sale.

When the **Protection Board** decided Coranderrk should close, Wonga organised a protest march to Melbourne. In 1875, Wonga died, but Barak continued the fight to save Coranderrk.

In 1881, Barak led another march to Melbourne, and several years later he organised a **petition** to the government.

Barak died in 1903. In 1924, Coranderrk was closed and the remaining people living there moved to Gippsland, Victoria.

People who lived at Coranderrk had to wear European clothing.

Central Australia

In the early 1880s, the Arrernte people of central Australia **conflicted** with **pastoralists** who continually wanted more land for their stock. They also clashed with the local police, who were quick to blame the Aboriginal people for crimes.

The Arrernte People

Police officer Constable William Willshire's job was to protect the community. In 1884, Willshire took command of a group of Aboriginal police. Instead of looking after the Aboriginal people, Willshire killed many Arrernte people.

Frank Gillen operated the **telegraph station** at Alice Springs. Gillen befriended many of the Arrernte people. He had great respect for their traditions and customs. When it was claimed that Constable Willshire had murdered two Aboriginal men while they were sleeping, Gillen reported him. Willshire was sent to trial but he was found not guilty.

Recording Culture

Frank Gillen and a scientist called Baldwin Spencer were concerned that Aboriginal peoples were losing their traditions and connection with the land because of the arrival of Europeans. They recorded and filmed some of the Arrernte customs and ceremonies. They also collected tools and **artefacts** that would teach people about the Arrernte ways. Their records have helped save important traditions for future **generations**.

The Alice Springs Telegraph Station became an important meeting place where Frank Gillen befriended the Arrernte people.

Arrernte men from Central Australia, with their faces and bodies painted, ready for a ceremony

Torres Strait Islander Peoples

Torres Strait Islander peoples live on mainland Australia and on 18 islands in the Torres Strait. Their traditions and customs, which have been influenced by their closeness to Australia and New Guinea, are still passed down from **generation** to generation. Music, dance, wood carving and art are important parts of traditional Torres Strait Islander culture.

The Pearling Industry

Pearl shells were a valuable resource for trade. Aboriginal people in northern Australia and Torres Strait Islanders collected pearls well before European arrival.

When Europeans became interested in pearling in the 1860s, they introduced diseases that Torres Strait Islanders had no resistance to. The Europeans also employed Torres Strait Islanders as pearl divers for little or no wages. Diving was dangerous and many people died or had accidents.

Just 30 years after European arrival there, the Torres Strait Islander population had declined by about 50 per cent.

Eddie Mabo

In the 1980s, Eddie Mabo and a group of Torres Strait Islander people began a legal battle to claim ownership of their land on the island of Mer. In 1993, the *Native Title Act* was passed and Indigenous peoples throughout Australia were able to claim traditional rights to their lands.

Mabo Day Parade in Cairns, 2010

Eddie Mabo helped bring about the *Native Title Act*. However, he died before the case was settled and did not get to see the reward for his efforts.

The Stolen Generations

For over 60 years, **generations** of Aboriginal and Torres Strait Islander babies and children were taken from their families and forced to live in institutions or with families of European descent.

Government Policies

The government and religious organisations supported the removal of children from their families. They thought European people could care for the children better than their own parents and communities. Australia wanted Aboriginal peoples, Torres Strait Islander peoples and migrants to **assimilate**, which means to live like European people.

Impact on Families

Taking children from their families was a **devastating** experience for the children, their parents and their whole community. Many children never saw their parents again. Brothers and sisters were separated from one another. The impact on people's lives continues to be felt today.

Some people are still trying to find their families and to understand what happened to them and why.

Many people who were torn from their families suffered health problems, such as depression, and died at much younger ages than other Australians. These people lost their cultural identity and felt they didn't belong in either the European people's world or their Aboriginal communities.

The Apology

On 13 February 2008, former Prime Minister Kevin Rudd formally apologised to the Stolen Generations. He said:

We apologise especially for the removal of Aboriginal and Torres Strait Islander children from their families, their communities and their country. For the pain, suffering and hurt of these Stolen Generations, their descendants and for their families left behind, we say sorry.

Many Indigenous children were taken from their families and placed in **orphanages**.

Changing Attitudes

Aboriginal people continued to suffer from **discrimination** throughout most of the 20th century. The government still managed their affairs in the belief that they knew better. In the 1960s, Australians became more aware of how Aboriginal people were being treated. Australians looked at how South Africa and the United States treated their indigenous and non-white people and finally realised they had not been doing any better.

Turning Point

In 1967, a **referendum** was held by the Australian goverment. Ninety per cent of Australians voted to change the law to include Aboriginal and Torres Strait Islander peoples in the national **census**. Up to this point, Aboriginal and Torres Strait Islander people had not been included in Australia's population counts.

Some states had already allowed Aboriginal and Torres Strait Islander people to vote in government elections before this time. However, many people did not know they were allowed to vote.

By the mid 1960s, everyone had equal rights to vote in all states of Australia. Voting became **compulsory** for Aboriginal and Torres Strait Islander people in 1984.

First Peoples

Aboriginal and Torres Strait Islander peoples have finally been recognised as Australia's first peoples. A National Congress of Australia's First Peoples was launched in 2010. The National Congress aims to provide a voice for Aboriginal and Torres Strait Islander peoples and to look after their needs and future.

The Aboriginal flag was designed by Harold Thomas. The black represents the Aboriginal peoples; the red is the red earth, red ochre and the spiritual connection to the land; and the yellow represents the sun, the giver of life. The flag was officially proclaimed as an Australian flag in 1995.

The Torres Strait Islander flag was officially recognised in 1995. The green represents the land; the blue is the sea; the white represents peace; and the black represents the Torres Strait Islander peoples. It was designed by Bernard Namok from Thursday Island.

Appreciating Indigenous Culture

In the 21st century, Aboriginal and Torres Strait Islander peoples continue to enjoy and practise their culture. Although some languages and traditions have been lost, many important stories and cultural events are still passed on to new **generations**.

Artwork

Aboriginal and Torres Strait Islander people receive respect and interest for their **contemporary** and traditional artwork. Their history as artists goes back a long way. Many **archaeological** discoveries of rock art and engravings are now protected, as are middens and ceremonial sites that have been uncovered.

Land and Sacred Sites

Uluru is one of the **sacred** sites that has been handed back to the traditional owners. Generations of the Anangu have looked after Uluru and the surrounding Country, using traditional practices and knowledge that has been passed down to them.

Uluru has great cultural importance, and the Anangu people ask that people do not climb this sacred site.

Astronomers

Aboriginal peoples are also being recognised as some of the world's first astronomers. The night sky was very important to traditional Aboriginal peoples.

An egg-shaped standing stone arrangement called Wurdi Youang discovered in Victoria demonstrates their interest in and knowledge of **astronomy**. It is the first astronomical site to be discovered in Australia, and it is possible that it was made before the pyramids in Egypt and Stonehenge in England.

The stone arrangement Wurdi Youang, near Geelong, Victoria

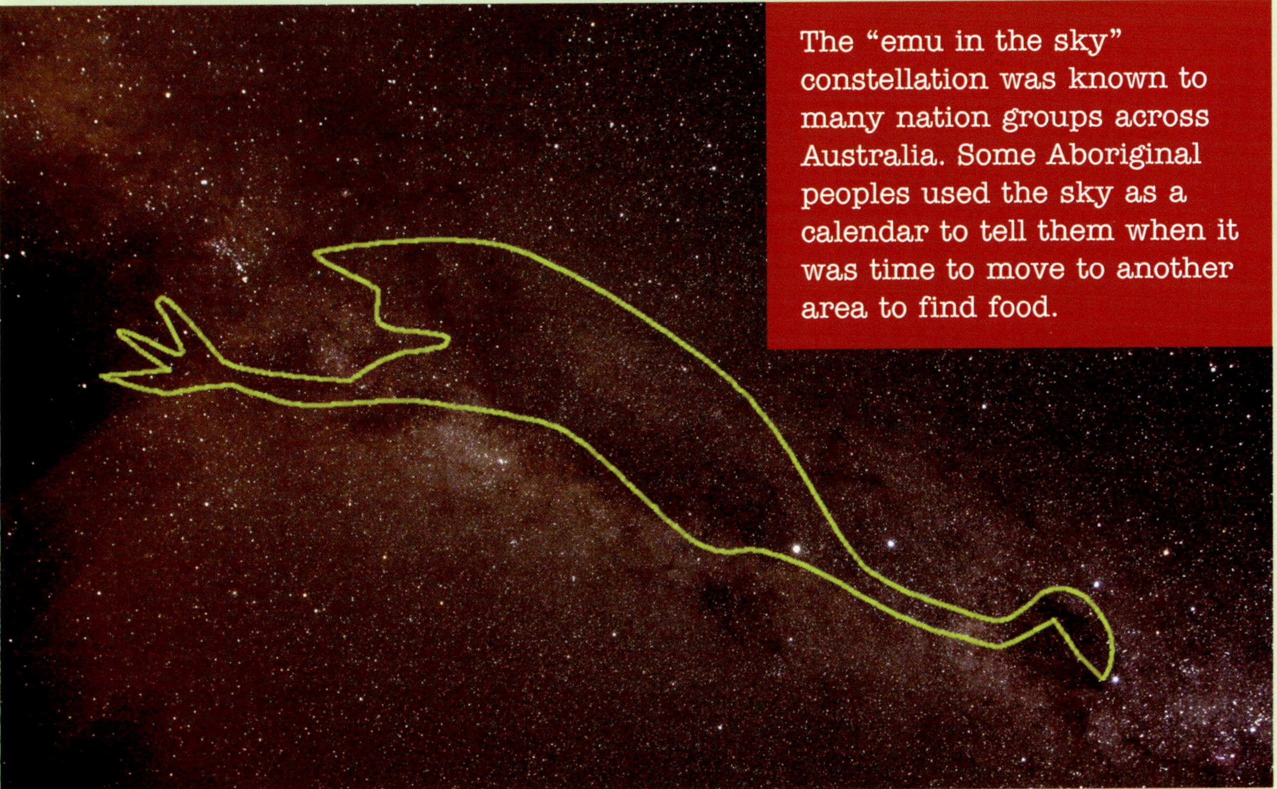

The "emu in the sky" constellation was known to many nation groups across Australia. Some Aboriginal peoples used the sky as a calendar to tell them when it was time to move to another area to find food.

Meet David Tournier

David Tournier is a proud member of the Wathaurong community. David is the Cultural **Heritage** Education Language Officer for the Wathaurong people, who traditionally lived in and around Geelong, Victoria.

The Kulin People

The Wathaurong people are part of the Kulin nation. Traditionally, the five groups making up the Kulin nation were different from each other, but had strong community links. The **clans** gathered together for trade and ceremonies.

The Kulin have two **moieties**—Bundjil is in the form of a wedge-tailed eagle and Waa is in the form of a crow or raven.

The raven is a Kulin moiety.

Cultural Links

David teaches people about the Wathaurong community, so they have a better understanding of Aboriginal peoples and the issues they face today. David is proud of his Aboriginal heritage. Part of his work involves helping Aboriginal people to stay connected to their own cultural heritage.

David teaches people about the healthy plants the Wathaurong people ate and lifestyles they had before European arrival.

Language

Aboriginal languages were traditionally spoken and not written down. David is keen to encourage the use of the traditional local language. He shares stories, language and his knowledge of his culture with children by writing traditional stories in the Wathaurong language. *Kim barne barre Wathaurong* translates to "This is Wathaurong Country". *Kungadgee* means "goodbye".

Meet Travis Varcoe

Travis Varcoe is an AFL footballer who plays for the Geelong Cats, the 2011 premiership team. Travis comes from Elizabeth in Adelaide. His traditional language group is Kaurna.

A Father's Advice

Travis's father encouraged him, his brother and two sisters to finish their education. Many children from Travis's suburb where he lived did not finish their schooling or have jobs. Travis took his father's advice.

AFL

Travis watched his first game of football when he was about seven years old. His cousin was playing for the Sydney Swans. Travis remembers being impressed that one of his relatives was playing **elite** football.

Travis played his first game of football when he was eight years old. He played a few games for the South Australian league and later played an international rules game in Ireland when he was 17 years old.

The Geelong Cats

Travis's first game for the Cats was in 2007. One of the highlights of his career has been running footy clinics for Aboriginal children in remote areas in the Northern Territory. Travis and his club promote healthy lifestyles and talk to children about the importance of attending school.

Travis believes that football and sport are powerful tools for Aboriginal people that can help them live happy and healthy lives. His connection with Aboriginal communities has benefited the children and helped to encourage them to attend school.

Travis is very proud of his Aboriginal **heritage**. His success as an AFL star has inspired many Aboriginal children to follow their dreams.

Timeline

60 000–50 000 years ago	Aboriginal people arrive in Australia from South-East Asia.
1778	The First Fleet arrives in New South Wales.
1800	The Aboriginal population is rapidly declining.
1803–1832	The Black War occurs against Tasmanian Aboriginal peoples.
1812	Truganini is born.
1828	Only approximately a few hundred Aboriginal people remain in Tasmania.
1830	A **bounty** is put on Aboriginal people and the Black Line is drawn to catch and kill Aboriginal people.
1835	The Aboriginal population in Victoria is estimated to be approximately 11 500.
1847	The government moves 47 people from the Flinders Island **mission** to the Tasmanian mainland.
1857	The Aboriginal population in Victoria is estimated to be less than 2000.
1860s	Europeans begin organised pearling in the Torres Strait Islands.
1868	Simon Wonga leads his people to Coranderrk to set up a reserve.
1875	Wonga dies.
1876	Truganini dies.

1904 Truganini's body is put on display in the Tasmanian Museum.

1906 Aboriginal people in the Great Sandy Desert in Western Australia meet Europeans for what is likely the first time.

1924 Coranderrk closes.

1967 Australia votes to include Aboriginal and Torres Strait Islander people in the **census**.

1976 Truganini's body is returned to her people.

1980s Eddie Mabo and a group of Torres Strait Islander people begin a legal battle to claim ownership of their land.

1984 Voting becomes **compulsory** for Aboriginal and Torres Strait Islander people.

1993 The *Native Title Act* recognises the land rights of Aboriginal and Torres Strait Islander peoples.

1995 The Aboriginal and Torres Strait Islander flags are officially recognised.

2002 Truganini's hair and skin are returned from Britain.

2008 Former Prime Minister Kevin Rudd officially apologises to the Stolen **Generations**.

2010 The National Congress of Australia's First Peoples forms.

Glossary

abundant plentiful or a large amount (for example, fruit or vegetables are abundant when they are in season)

ancestors relatives that people have descended from (for example, parents, grandparents, great-grandparents)

ancient happening long ago

archaeological relating to the study of sites where remains of ancient civilisations have been discovered

artefacts objects from long ago made by people

assimilate to take on the same customs and lifestyles of a culture or community

astronomy the study of stars and planets

bounty a reward of money for doing something

campaign a planned series of actions to achieve something

census an official count of the population (made every four years in Australia)

clan a family group. In traditional Aboriginal society, clan members lived together and shared food and other resources.

compulsory must be done; not optional

conflicted clashed over or disagreed over (something)

contemporary modern

continent one of the seven great land masses of Earth such as Australia, Africa and North America

decimated wiped out

devastating shocking or upsetting

discrimination treating people unfairly because of, for example, their race, sex or religion

elite at the top level

generations stages in a family, such as children, parents and grandparents

heritage things that someone has inherited, such as customs or traditions

life expectancy the average age that a person is likely to live to

massacres the killing of large numbers of people at once

mission a place where missionaries work. Many Aboriginal people lived in missions, where they were converted to Christianity.

moieties groups in Aboriginal culture that have spiritual importance

outlawed excluded from legal rights and the protection of the law

pastoralists farmers; graziers

petition a statement of appeal or request and a list of signatures supporting it

petitioned asked or requested

Protection Board a board set up to manage the lives of Aboriginal people

reclaimed to have claimed or got back something owned previously

referendum a vote by people of a nation on a particular topic or question put forward by the government

sacred of spiritual importance

spokesperson a person who speaks for a group of people

telegraph station a place where the messages from a telegraph line connected to other places are received

Index